W9-DFM-280

THE MAGIC OF LANGUAGE

Conjunctions

By Ann Heinrichs

THE CHILD'S WORLD®
CHANHASSEN, MINNESOTA

Published in the United States of America by The Child's World®
PO Box 326, Chanhassen, MN 55317-0326
800-599-READ
www.childsworld.com

Content Adviser:
Kathy Rzany, M.A.,
Adjunct Professor,
School of Education,
Dominican University,
River Forest, Illinois

Photo Credits: Cover photograph: Punchstock/RubberBall Interior photographs:
Animals Animals/Earth Scenes: 5 (Charles Palek), 8 (Roger de la Harpe), 22 (Ruth
Cole); Corbis: 7, 11 (Brent Bear); Getty Images/The Image Bank: 13 (James Balog),
17 (Marc Romanelli), 19 (G. K. & Vikki Hart); Getty Images/PhotoDisc/Michael
Lamotte/Cole Group: 29; Punchstock: 15 (Digital Vision), 24 (BananaStock);
Stockbyte/PictureQuest: 25.

The Child's World®: Mary Berendes, Publishing Director

Editorial Directions, Inc.: E. Russell Primm, Editorial Director; Pam Rosenberg,
Project Editor; Melissa McDaniel, Line Editor; Katie Marsico, Assistant Editor;
Matt Messbarger, Editorial Assistant; Susan Hindman, Copyeditor; Susan Ashley and
Sarah E. De Capua, Proofreaders; Chris Simms and Olivia Nellums, Fact Checkers;
Timothy Griffin/IndexServ, Indexer; Cian Loughlin O'Day and Dawn Friedman,
Photo Researchers; Linda S. Koutris, Photo Selector

The Design Lab: Kathleen Petelinsek, Design and Page Production;
Kari Thornborough, Page Production Assistant

Library of Congress Cataloging-in-Publication Data
Heinrichs, Ann.
  Conjunctions / by Ann Heinrichs.
    p. cm. — (The magic of language)
Includes index.
Contents: What is a conjunction?—A sandwich and a house? No way!—And, and,
and,—Laughing at chimpanzees—Conjunction twins—Conjunctive adverbs—Acting
like a conjunction—Because why? Since when?—As if! Another tricky conjunction—
Just for fun : sloppy conjunctions.
  ISBN 1-59296-071-5 (library bound : alk. paper)
  1. English language—Conjunctions—Juvenile literature. [1. English language—
Conjunctions.] I. Title. II. Series: The Magic of Language.
  PE1345.H45 2004
  428.2—dc22   20030200690

TABLE OF CONTENTS

CHAPTER ONE

WHAT IS A CONJUNCTION?

DEFINITION

A **conjunction** is a word that connects two or more words or word groups.

Conjunctions are like glue. They stick words together. We'd be lost without them! Just look at these examples. The blue words are conjunctions. Imagine each sentence without its conjunction.

EXAMPLE

Gorillas are huge **but** friendly.
We won the game **and** walked away with the trophy.
Pass the potatoes **unless** they're too hot.
Is Sparky in his doghouse **or** on my bed?

The conjunctions you know best are **and, or,** and **but.** But you'll soon see that there are plenty of others. **Although,**

because, until,

besides, mean-

while, and **otherwise**

are all conjunctions.

Most conjunctions are

just one word. However,

two or more words can act

together as a conjunction.

Even though, in

fact, for example,

and **on the other hand**

all act as conjunctions. Now

let's have some fun with these

useful words!

Until the gorilla decides what to have for lunch, he will be hungry and his stomach will growl. How many conjunctions are in the previous sentence? If you found two, then you are right!

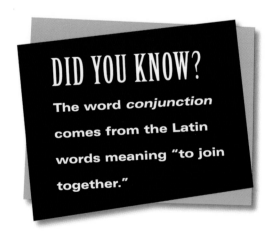

DID YOU KNOW?

The word *conjunction* comes from the Latin words meaning "to join together."

CHAPTER TWO

A SANDWICH AND A HOUSE?
NO WAY!

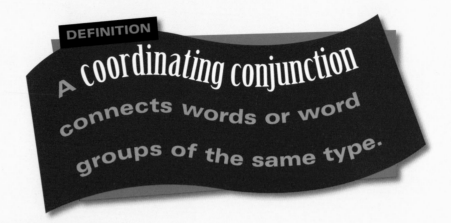

DEFINITION

A **coordinating conjunction** connects words or word groups of the same type.

Would you wear one shoe and an airplane to school? Would you carry a sandwich and a house in your lunch box? Of course not! You'd wear two shoes or two boots. Your lunch box might have a sandwich and an apple in it. You'd keep the same kinds of things together.

Coordinating conjunctions work the same way. They join words or word groups of the same kind. For example, they can join words, such as two nouns or two verbs.

*Nothing goes together quite as well as peanut butter and jelly.
The conjunctive **and** helps bring them together!*

NOUNS   Can Sarah or Ryan come over today?

VERBS   Nathaniel tossed and turned all night long.

ADJECTIVES   Lizards can be green or brown.

ADVERBS   Snoopy snored peacefully yet loudly.

Coordinating conjunctions can join phrases, too.

My goldfish jumped out of its tank and into my shoe.
Then it sprang out of my shoe and through
the window!

When joining words or phrases, coordinating conjunctions give us a shorter, easier way to say things. We don't have to repeat extra words. Just look at all the extra words in these examples:

Lizards can be green, or lizards can be brown.
Snoopy snored peacefully, yet Snoopy snored loudly.
It sprang out of my shoe, and it sprang through
the window!

*This lizard has green and black skin. The coordinating conjunction **and** helps us describe this animal.*

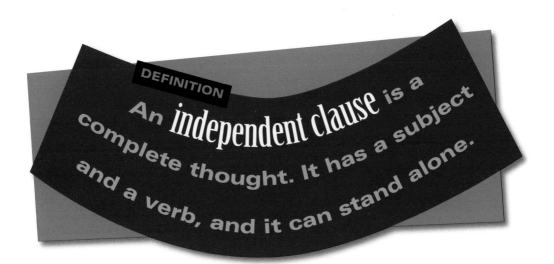

Coordinating conjunctions can also join independent clauses.

Independent clauses are complete thoughts. They are equally important, and they can stand alone. Remove the conjunction, and both clauses still make sense.

EXAMPLE

Brian has 40 baseball cards, but Eric has 50.
Brian has 40 baseball cards. Eric has 50.

Usually you separate the clauses with a comma. However, if the clauses are very short, you don't need a comma.

EXAMPLE

Roses are red and violets are blue.
Shape up or ship out!
Close the door but don't slam it.

CHAPTER THREE

AND . . . AND . . . AND . . .

EXAMPLE

I'll have mustard and ketchup and pickles and relish and peppers and onions, please!

Did you ever order a hot dog or hamburger this way? If you did, you must have run out of breath! You don't need to keep repeating the conjunction. Instead, separate the items with commas.

Then put the conjunction before the last item.

EXAMPLE

I'll have mustard, ketchup, pickles, relish, peppers, and onions, please!

But wait! Sometimes you *want* to repeat the conjunction. You do this to make sure the listener gets your message!

EXAMPLE

That terrier of yours just barks and barks and barks!

Maybe you enjoy lots of different things on your hot dog, but you only
need to use one conjunction when you order all of them.

CHAPTER FOUR

LAUGHING AT CHIMPANZEES

DEFINITION

A subordinating conjunction connects a main clause with a dependent clause.

EXAMPLE

I laugh whenever I see chimpanzees.

In this sentence, **whenever** is a subordinating conjunction.

We simply cannot do without this word! Remove the conjunc-

tion, and here's what you have:

EXAMPLE

I laugh. I see chimpanzees.

Fine. You're laughing. You see chimpanzees. But what's the

connection? The missing link is **whenever!**

A subordinating conjunction connects two clauses. These two

clauses are not the same kind of clause. One is the main clause.

It's an independent clause that can stand alone. In the example

above, I laugh is the main clause.

DEFINITION

A **dependent clause** has a subject and a verb. However, it's not a complete thought, and it can't stand alone.

The subordinating conjunction intro-

duces the other clause—the dependent

clause. The dependent clause hangs

onto, or depends on, the main

clause. Whenever I see chim-

panzees is the dependent clause.

The dependent clause can come

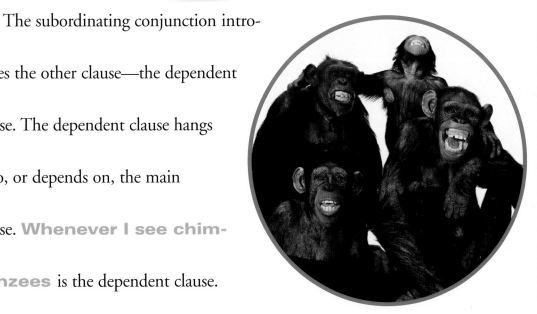

*Do you crack up whenever you see chimpanzees acting silly? The subordinating conjunction **whenever** links the reason you're laughing with the goofy chimps.*

before or after the main clause. Either way, the conjunction must be *at the beginning* of the dependent clause. In the example below, the main clause is still **I laugh,** but there are two dependent clauses.

One is before the main clause, and one is after it.

EXAMPLE

Whenever I see chimpanzees, I laugh **until** my sides ache.

Want More?

Here are some common subordinating conjunctions: **after, although, because, before, if, so, unless, until, when, whenever, while.**

TRY THESE!

Use **subordinating conjunctions** to connect these clauses. Point out which is the main clause and which is the dependent clause.

1. The rooster always crows. The sun rises.
2. I'll be home at eight. I can get a ride.
3. I read comics. I howl. My friends cover their ears.

See page 32 for the answers. Don't peek!

*We all know that roosters crow, and we also know that the sun rises. What's the connection? Roosters crow when the sun rises. The word **when** is the subordinating conjunction that helps us link the two thoughts in a single sentence!*

CHAPTER FIVE

CONJUNCTION TWINS

DEFINITION

Correlative conjunctions
are conjunctions that work together in pairs.

Do you know any twins? If you do, you know they may not

be exactly alike. But they do come in pairs.

Correlative conjunctions are like word twins.

They come in pairs, too. Correlative conjunc-

tions include **both/and, either/or,**

neither/nor, not/but,

not only/but also,

and **whether/or.**

HOT TIP

Here's an easy way to remember that correlative conjunctions come in pairs. Part of the word correlative is relative. Just think of twins—they're relatives!

Like coordinating conjunctions, correlative conjunctions join things that are alike. They may join two words, two phrases, or two clauses.

*If we say that either Andy will get a home run or we will lose the game, we are using the **either/or** correlative conjunction.*

EXAMPLE

Both parrots **and** sloths live in South America.

Neither zebras **nor** giraffes live in Asia.

Father Goose is **not** a goose **but** a gander.

I can't decide **whether** to do my homework **or** to go to bed.

James **either** makes a double play **or** hits a home run.

That ball landed **either** on the roof **or** in the pond.

Julie **not only** wrote the book **but also** directed the movie.

Either I get my pie, **or** I go home!

CHAPTER SIX

CONJUNCTIVE ADVERBS

DEFINITION

A **conjunctive adverb** joins two independent clauses. It shows a relationship between the clauses and helps them flow smoothly.

T wo independent clauses can stand alone, each as a complete thought. Then what does the conjunctive adverb do? For one thing, it helps you move smoothly from one idea to another. Things could sound pretty choppy without it!

DID YOU KNOW?

A conjunctive adverb is sometimes called an adverbial conjunction.

Conjunctive adverbs also show some special relationship between the two clauses. They might compare, sum up, or help make a point.

I love cherries; in fact, I ate a whole bucketful.

Bozo had everyone in stitches. In short, he was a
   big success.

Our turtle started last; so far, he's still behind.

Jose is very athletic; his sister also loves sports.

Horses are fun to ride. I prefer camels, however.

As you see, there are two ways to separate the clauses. One way

is with a semicolon (;). A semicolon works well when the clauses are

short. You can also make the clauses into two separate sentences, with

a conjunctive adverb in the second one.

This turtle and rabbit are having a race; so far, it looks like they are tied!
*In this sentence, **so far** is the conjunctive adverb.*

Where does the conjunctive adverb go? It can appear in many places. Often it's at the beginning of the clause it introduces. However, it can sometimes occur at the end of the clause—or even in the middle.

Want More?

Here are some common conjunctive adverbs: **after all, again, also, anyway, besides, certainly, even though, eventually, finally, for example, furthermore, however, in fact, likewise, meanwhile, nevertheless, of course, otherwise, so far, therefore, though, thus.**

TRY THESE!

Here are four pairs of clauses. See how choppy they sound? Fix them by using a conjunctive adverb to connect each pair.

1. **Sparky never bites. He growls a lot.**
2. **My feet aren't cold. It's still summer.**
3. **You have all the cards. You win.**
4. **Shut the door. Bugs will get in.**

See page 32 for the answers. Don't peek!

CHAPTER SEVEN

ACTING LIKE A CONJUNCTION

Some words can be either prepositions or subordinating conjunctions. They are before, after, and until. How can you tell which is which? Just remember two simple rules:

(1) Every preposition has an object.

(2) A subordinating conjunction introduces a dependent clause.

EXAMPLE

PREPOSITION   We're cranky before bedtime.
CONJUNCTION   We're cranky before we get our pizza.

PREPOSITION   Meet me after lunch.
CONJUNCTION   Meet me after I clean my desk.

PREPOSITION   I shall wait until noon.
CONJUNCTION   I shall wait until the cows come home.

That is another word with many uses. It can be a pronoun, an adjective, or even an adverb. Just look:

*We think that this monkey looks sad. In this sentence, **that** is the subordinating conjunction because it introduces the dependent clause.*

PRONOUN   **That** belongs to me.

ADJECTIVE **That** monkey belongs to me.

ADVERB   Its tail is not **that** long.

That can act as a subordinating conjunction, too. It introduces a dependent clause.

EXAMPLE

Ms. Lopez announced **that** everyone could leave at noon.

Don't forget **that** we have rehearsal tonight.

Sometimes you can leave **that** out, and the sentence still makes sense.

EXAMPLE

Sophie knew **(that)** she'd written a good poem.

Be glad **(that)** you are here.

CHAPTER EIGHT

BECAUSE WHY?
SINCE WHEN?

Some conjunctions can be tricky. They might trick you into using the wrong word. For example, you might use **since** when you really mean **because.** So let's be tricky, too! Just follow some simple rules.

Use **because** to show a reason. **Because** answers the question "why?"

EXAMPLE

> We haven't seen Grandpa **because** he's out of town.
> Hannah has been wearing her new outfit **because** she loves it.
> Skeeter doesn't bark **because** he's too tired.

Use **since** to show a certain point in time. **Since** answers the question "when?"

EXAMPLE

We haven't seen Grandpa since he got home.

Hannah has been wearing her new outfit since she got it.

Skeeter doesn't bark since we changed his dog food.

*This little girl looks happy because she's wearing her new dress. The word **because** tells the reader why she is happy.*

TRY THESE!

Fill in the blanks with because or since.

1. We haven't eaten _____ the sun went down.

2. I couldn't sleep _____ the lights were too bright.

3. Poopsie keeps meowing _____ she sees a bird.

4. Elephants haven't come here _____ their water hole dried up.

See page 32 for the answers. Don't peek!

CHAPTER NINE

AS IF! ANOTHER TRICKY CONJUNCTION

Want another tricky conjunction? **As if!** Yes, it's true—**as if** is a subordinating conjunction. It introduces a dependent clause. **As if** answers the question "how?"

EXAMPLE

> We screamed **as if** we'd seen a ghost.
> It seemed **as if** class would
>   never end.
> It looks **as if** it's going
>   to rain.

What's the tricky part? **As if** is often confused with **like.** However, **like** is a preposition. As with all prepositions, **like** only has an object. It doesn't introduce a clause.

*Have you ever felt as if your school day would never end? The subordinating conjunction **as if** introduces a dependent clause.*

WRONG	It seemed like class would never end.
RIGHT	It seemed like a movie.

WRONG	It looks like it's going to rain
RIGHT	It looks like a trick.

WRONG	We screamed like we'd seen a ghost.
RIGHT	We screamed like fire engines.

HOT TIP

As if introduces a clause. Like never introduces a clause.

TRY THESE!

Fill in the blanks with as if or like.

1. Act _____ a gorilla.

2. Act _____ you want to be chosen.

3. I ran _____ tigers were chasing me.

4. I ran _____ the wind.

See page 32 for the answers. Don't peek!

CHAPTER TEN

JUST FOR FUN: SLOPPY CONJUNCTIONS

EXAMPLE

Jennifer is friendly **and** Jennifer is polite.

Scooter is black **and** Scooter is gray.

That mouse grabbed the cheese

    and grabbed the nuts!

Whew! That's a lot of extra words!

Remember the coordinating conjunctions? They can give us a

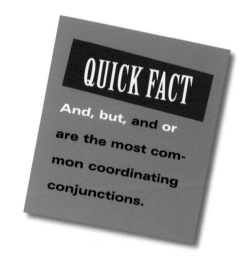

QUICK FACT

And, but, and or are the most common coordinating conjunctions.

shorter, easier way to say things. We don't have to repeat extra words.

Get rid of the extra words, and the meaning stays the same.

EXAMPLE

Jennifer is friendly **and** polite.

Scooter is black **and** gray.

That mouse grabbed the cheese **and** the nuts!

Now look at these examples:

EXAMPLE

Eat these brownies while they're nice and hot.

I'll try and get a B on my math test.

We'll stop reading when we're good and ready!

Are these shorter and easier ways to say something? Let's find out

by adding in the extra words:

EXAMPLE

Eat these brownies while they're nice and while they're hot.

I'll try and I'll get a B on my math test.

We'll stop reading when we're good and when we're ready!

Oops! These sentences are not what we mean at all! What's the

problem? We got a little sloppy with the coordinating conjunction

and. It didn't pass the "extra words" test!

It's easy and fun to say nice and hot, try and get, and

good and ready. But remember—these words don't say what

Eat these brownies while they're really hot, and be sure to avoid using sloppy conjunctions!

you really mean. How can you fix them? Just remove the sloppy

conjunction and use different words!

EXAMPLE

Eat these brownies while they're really hot.
I'll try to get a B on my math test.
We'll stop reading when we're absolutely ready!

How to Learn More

At the Library

Collins, S. Harold, and Kathy Kifer (illustrator). *Prepositions, Conjunctions, and Interjections.* Eugene, Ore.: Garlic Press, 1992.

Heller, Ruth. *Fantastic! Wow! and Unreal!: A Book about Interjections and Conjunctions.* New York: Grosset & Dunlap, 1998.

Terban, Marvin, and Peter Spacek (illustrator). *Checking Your Grammar.* New York: Scholastic, 1994.

Usborne Books. *Prepositions and Conjunctions.* Tulsa, Okla.: EDC Publications, 1999.

On the Web

Visit our home page for lots of links about grammar:

http://www.childsworld.com/links.html

NOTE TO PARENTS, TEACHERS AND LIBRARIANS: We routinely check our Web links to make sure they're safe, active sites—so encourage your readers to check them out!

Through the Mail or by Phone

To find a Grammar Hotline near you, contact:

THE GRAMMAR HOTLINE DIRECTORY
Tidewater Community College Writing Center
1700 College Crescent
Virginia Beach, VA 23453
Telephone: (757) 822-7170
http://www.tcc.edu/students/resources/writcent/GH/hotlino1/htm

To learn more about grammar, visit the Grammar Lady
online or call her toll free hotline:

THE GRAMMAR LADY
Telephone: (800) 279-9708
www.grammarlady.com

Fun with Conjunctions

Subordinating conjunctions can completely change the meaning of a sentence. Read each of these sentences twice, using a different conjunction each time. Tell how the meaning is different each time.

I want to swim until/while I eat lunch.

Emily will go because/unless I am going.

Brush your teeth before/after you go to bed.

Although/Because he is a clown, he is sad.

My hands get dirty if/so I wash them.

Index

Answers

Answers to Text Exercises
page 14

There are many possible answers. Here are some suggestions. *(The main clause is in italics.)*

1. *The rooster always crows* before the sun rises.

2. *I'll be home at eight* if I can get a ride.

3. When I read comics, *I howl* until my friends cover their ears.

page 20

There are many possible answers. Here are some suggestions:

1. Sparky never bites; nevertheless, he growls a lot.

2. My feet aren't cold. After all, it's still summer.

3. You have all the cards; therefore, you win.

4. Shut the door; otherwise, bugs will get in.

page 24
1. since
2. because
3. because
4. since

page 26
1. like
2. as if
3. as if
4. like

About the Author

Ann Heinrichs was lucky. Every year from grade three through grade eight, she had a big, fat grammar text-book and a grammar workbook. She feels that this prepared her for life. She is now the author of more than 100 books for children and young adults. She has also enjoyed successful careers as a children's book editor and an advertising copywriter. Ann grew up in Fort Smith, Arkansas, and lives in Chicago, Illinois.